it's NOT a load of RUBBiSH

Written by Caren Trafford

Illustrations by
David Wilsher
and Jessica Laurentia

The Gang

DUMPI... a crumpled, chatty paper bag, who's come clean with his knowledge on waste and recycling. He's on a mission to win a gold medal for being the most recycled bag on the planet.

MIKEY THE MUNCHING MICROBE... a very small, extremely hungry, munching microbe. He's one of trillions of microbes hanging around this great big planet, munching his way every day, through all that chucked muck.

DIG-IT... the inquisitive archaeologist. Always on the scent, Dig-it likes to dig deep to the roots and spends days sifting through odds and sods, uncovering what's gone down.

WASTE-NOT and **WANT-NOT...** the twin roo-lers of the tip. They think that every tale needs a good punch and are standing by to dish the dirt.

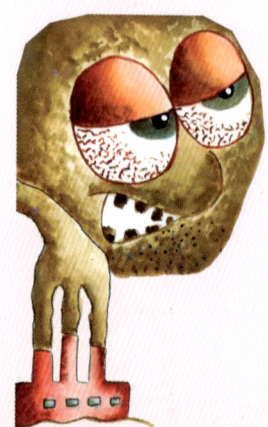

POO-LOOTER... out to loot the planet of its natural resources - he's got a thing or two to say about the state of play. Can you convince him that he's got it all wrong?

Published by Etram Pty Ltd
www.planetkids.biz

First published in Australia 2006
2nd Edition 2006

Copyright
Text © Caren Trafford 2006 &
Illustrations
© Caren Trafford 2006

All rights reserved. No part of this publication may be reproduced, stored in a retrieval system, or transmitted in any form or by any means, electronic, mechanical, photocopying, recorded, or otherwise, without the prior written permission of the copyright owner.

National Library of Australia Cataloguing-in-Publisher entry:
Trafford, Caren
World Wide Waste...
It's Not a Load of Rubbish
ISBN 0-9581878-2-7

Illustrator: David Wilsher & Jessica Laurentia
Design: Serious Business
Printed in China through Bookbuilders

Time to Come Clean

World **W**ide **W**aste… it might sound like a pile of old rubbish, but out there is a huge heap of trash wanting to be famous. It didn't take a lot of digging to sniff out this great interview; full of cover-ups, bad smells, danger, destruction and the quest to save the planet. Meet the gang who've dug the dirt and wasted no time to bring you the incredible story, 'Coming clean in the 21st century'.

Meet the bag that's not just full of hot air

You wouldn't normally listen to a brown paper bag - even a very intelligent one with a passion for rapping - but Dumpi's not just full of rhythm and hot air. He knows that even if you walk the walk and talk the talk, you still might not get it. The truth is… there's no such thing as waste.

*Down on the street,
when you listen to the beat,
don't take a load of heat - be neat,
move those feet and you'll be sweet.*

Here's Dumpi's deal. The meaning of life, hip-hop and the universe is simple - everything is recyclable; if it isn't, it should be.

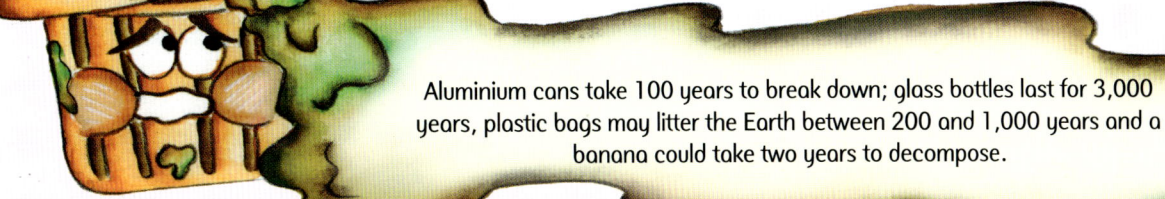

Aluminium cans take 100 years to break down; glass bottles last for 3,000 years, plastic bags may litter the Earth between 200 and 1,000 years and a banana could take two years to decompose.

Welcome to Recycling 101...

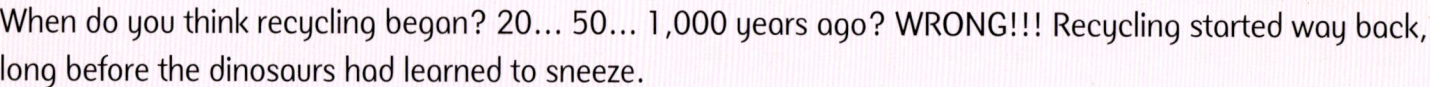

Let's start at the very beginning.

When do you think recycling began? 20... 50... 1,000 years ago? WRONG!!! Recycling started way back, long before the dinosaurs had learned to sneeze.

In nature, there's no such thing as waste. As soon as one use finishes, another begins. Recycling is Nature's way of cleaning up the world; *she likes looking good*. All life, from the earliest single cell organisms, to today's huge variety of plants and animals, is part of one giant recycling circle.

Early supermarkets sold a wide range of organic products

Take soil. It doesn't grow in the garden, it's the result of living organisms and minerals being recycled.

This planet has been recycling, reworking and relocating its rubbish and waste, quite naturally, for millions of years: whether it's a volcano spewing millions of tonnes of ash, oceans moving great quantities of sand across sea-beds, or rivers grinding down mountains and carving canyons.

Nature's *Super Cycle* is one of the most powerful forces on the planet. If recycling didn't occur naturally, you'd be up to your necks in mountains of leaves, piles of poo and rivers of rubbish.

Our world would be a very different place if Nature wasn't such a super-sorter.

The Big Chew

How does Nature's *Super Cycle* work without giant machines? Mother Earth can't put out her recycling bins for some giant space truck to collect each week.

The answer's almost invisible and it's right under your nose. 'MMM' a.k.a 'Millions of Munching Microbes,' are the way world-wide waste is kept under control.

Microbes are tiny, microscopic critters, thought to be one of the world's oldest life-forms.

Someone close to the ground is Mikey the Munching Microbe. He can tell you that microbes are always hungry and love to munch on almost anything. It's a form of global happiness! Nature gets all her recycling done and microbes get a free feed.

How do munching microbes make room for dessert?

Bacteria are one of the teeniest microbes who love eating waste. Some munch on oil and petrol, cleaning up polluted lakes and rivers - a great way to make underwater friends.

Other bacteria, *(probably those who get sea-sick)* prefer to munch on dry land and 'eat' anything from sugar and starch to sulphur and iron.

There are some very clever bacteria that can do two things at once - eat pollution and generate electricity. However, the award for the most amazing bacteria goes to the ones that can eat human sewage and turn it into rocket fuel. *How many of your friends can do that?*

Who are you calling a bright spark?

Bacteria aren't the only critters that love to eat waste. Hundreds of insects and worms, munch their way through lunch - Nature's waste - every day. Under proper conditions, these creatures can reduce piles of waste into rich, fertile soil.

Really hungry compost worms can eat their weight in waste a day. *Imagine an elephant doing that!* Have you ever looked at a worm's bottom? What comes out is worm poo, or vermicast - the perfect food for plants.

Microbes, insects, and worms aren't afraid of hard work. When scientists wanted to clean the bones of a 12 metre whale, they buried the skeleton, still covered with flesh, in horse manure for a whole year. When they dug it up, they discovered that the bacteria and insects had cleaned the bones perfectly. *Go the Bugs!!*

Do microbes get tummy-aches if they don't chew their food?

Early Droppings

It's so uncool to leave rubbish lying around, but take a peek at history - humans have been doing it for centuries.

In ancient times, people lived in small groups, and moved from place to place with the changing seasons. Their waste; ash from burnt fires, bones, bodies and vegetable scraps, was just left on the ground.

When things piled up you could just move on

Later, when these hunter-gatherers settled and began to farm, they built villages and towns and adopted an *'out of sight... out of mind'* attitude towards their rubbish. They *'chucked their muck,'* and *'trashed their stash,'* into the nearest river or dropped it down a hole or pit. When one hole filled up, they dug another one.

As early as 3,000 BC, in Knossos, the Cretan capital, waste was placed in large pits and covered with earth. By 2,000 BC, composting was part of life in ancient China, but at the same time, the Ancient Egyptians collected and dumped their waste into the Nile River. *Perhaps that's why it flooded each year?*

The Greek, Roman and Moorish Empires shared and recycled architectural ideas and often built temples, fortresses and garrisons from recycled stone and wood.

The early empires didn't let rubbish pile up under their feet. Records show that by 500 BC, Athens had municipal dumps, compost piles and laws that decreed waste had to be dumped at least one mile from the city walls.

Chariot competitions may have started as a race to the city dump

7

Dumpi-astotle the well-known *poo-losopher*, wrote widely on the subject of rubbish removal.

'*Can't think if it stinks,*' was one of his favorite sayings.

'What a load of rubbish,' was a common phrase in the market-place

Expanding the early empires would have been impossible without large fleets of ships and much of the material used in ship-building was recycled. Timber and iron nails were often re-used from one ship to the next. Iron was very valuable and a 25 metre ship would contain thousands of nails.

The pirates that roamed the seven seas had their own version of recycling and made sure that any treasures they captured did not go to waste. *Shiver me timbers*!

Many metals were recycled as money, jewellery, weapons, containers and cooking pots. Of course, no-one ever threw gold away. It could be melted down and re-cast. The same was true of bronze, silver, tin and copper.

Walking the plank is one way to get rid of any old rubbish

The Big Stink

By the 11th century, most of the great ideas on waste collection and recycling had been forgotten. More than 80 universities existed in Europe, but there wasn't a single course on, 'Where to chuck your muck.'

Rubbish ruled everywhere: it was burnt at home on open fires, tossed out onto the streets and when it got too disgusting outside the front door, you could always *fling your dung* or *shove your stuff*, out of the back door.

Animals lived in the bedroom and your pig or dog might be the four-legged waste-disposal system for the whole neighbourhood.

Mountains of trash attracted rats, carrying disease and plague. Bubonic plague, known also as the Black Death, broke out in 1350. In three years, it killed one-third of the people in Europe.

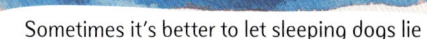
Sometimes it's better to let sleeping dogs lie

By the 1800s, London had become the largest and most polluted city in the world. Cholera and typhoid outbreaks were frequent and the Thames River became so dirty that 1858 was referred to as the 'Year of the Big Stink'.

When the idea of recycling sewage was first introduced in England, it was rejected. Instead pipe systems were built, sending all that lovely nutrient they called waste, into the rivers and out to sea. *Wasting the waste... what a waste!*

Dogs' doo-doo was considered very valuable and tanners used it to soften leather. The name, 'dustmen' came from the 1800s when you could earn money by collecting the ash from coal fires and selling it as a soil conditioner or for brick-making.

Holes are Not Just For Moles

Today, humans can fly to the moon, build robots and invent computers but they still chuck their muck down big holes called landfills. Landfills are found near most large towns and cities and they're the places where rubbish goes to die. In the last twenty years the amount of waste thrown out has more than doubled. How much stuff that's chucked, do you think could be re-used or recycled? 20%... 30%? WRONG... a huge 60%!

Nowadays, landfills are designed to strict health and safety guidelines to stop toxic liquids leaking through and contaminating the groundwater. Gas-wells are often added to extract the methane gas, produced as waste breaks down.

The good news is that once a landfill is full, it can be covered and used for recreational activities. *Anyone for golf?* The bad news... landfills are the end of the road for all the rubbish that could have been recycled.

Waste-not and Want-not, our two roo landfill experts believe landfills should be reserved for wastes which can harm the environment. At the moment, all sorts of waste is thrown into these big holes. Old computers, radios, newspapers, clothing, food, boxes, plastics, paper, tyres, plus - don't forget the sauce - waste and sludge from sewage treatment plants.

Once buried, the waste materials decompose, but only very slowly. When scientists in the USA drilled down into a landfill, they discovered 30 year-old newspapers that they could still read.

Incineration or burning is an alternative way to get rid of waste, but this destroys raw materials that could be recycled and burning waste also produces acidic, greenhouse gases and toxic chemicals that must be treated with expensive pollution-control equipment.

Rubbish doesn't have to be wasted. Listen to Waste-not and Want-not – they'd love to punch some sense into those world-wide wasters.

It can take a while to digest all the news

Rubbish Dumps or Treasure Troves?

Digging for bones can be a life-long occupation

To help uncover this story, we've enlisted an expert, who specialises in sniffing out the facts. He's discovered that while some humans bury millions of tonnes of rubbish in landfill, others go to university to learn how to dig it up again.

Meet Dig-it – our favourite archaeologist. Have you ever seen an archaeologist at work? They spend many months digging for bits buried below the surface. When they discover something, *(which could take years,)* they clean it, call it an artifact, label it and put it into the museum.

According to Dig-it, archaeology is the study of ancient peoples and their cultures. Strange as it sounds, archaeologists go wild over the rubbish that ancient cultures left behind.

All sorts of things are found underground; weapons, cooking utensils, glass containers, pottery, tools, jewellery – even food. Archaeologists in Britain recently dug up some 5,500 year-old bread and in north-west China, 4,000 year-old spaghetti was found. *Anyone for left-overs?*

In the United Arab Emirates, a coffee bean dating from the 12th century was discovered. It is said to be the oldest coffee bean ever found. *Where's my espresso?*

Archaeologists like to keep a sharp eye on the ground

Archaeologists act like detectives, looking for clues on how people lived and what they ate and wore. From their finds, they try to reconstruct the diet, culture and even the economy of an area. *Do you think they practise detective-work on the garbage they take out at home?*

In Egypt, in 1922, the tomb of boy king Tutankhamun was unearthed in the Valley of the Kings. Considered to be one of the most exciting archaeological discoveries ever made, it contained over 3,000 treasures and gave the world a unique glimpse of royal Egyptian life 30 centuries ago.

It's not just archaeologists who dig things up. In the northern parts of China and Mongolia, a whole industry has grown up from unearthing and recycling the remains of woolly mammoths that died over 10,000 years ago. Their ivory tusks are worth many thousands of dollars.

There are many ways to lose your trousers - some are a little hard to believe

Not all archaeological quests lead to treasure, but many of the items thrown out and buried years ago reveal answers to our ancestors' daily lives.

Rubbish will try all sorts of tricks to stay away from the big black hole

From start to Finish or is it?

Everything you use is part of a bigger picture. Check out the life-cycle… how can you keep it in balance?

Extraction - Getting raw materials out of the ground affects the environment. Once extracted or removed, raw materials, like oil, coal or gas must be transformed into a usable form. This is an energy-intensive process that often results in air and water pollution and unwanted by-products.

Processing - The manufacturing of products like cars, clothes, fridges or phones, takes further processes which uses more energy and generates even more pollution.

Marketing - Once a product is finished it must be transported and stored before being sent to the shops. This uses up still more energy and more waste is created from the packaging, advertising and promotional materials. When you buy anything that needs petrol, gas, batteries or electricity, the production and use of these generates pollution.

Consumption - Whatever you've bought will eventually be thrown away. But really, there is no such thing as 'away'. After you throw it away, you may not see it anymore, but something still has to be done with it.

Disposal - If your waste is toxic or dangerous, like paint, batteries or cleaning materials, more resources and energy are used up disposing of it all safely. If your rubbish is incinerated or burnt, more pollution can be created and the incinerator ash may have to be carefully monitored for hundreds of years.

It seems that there are two choices: Never throw away anything again… or find something useful to do with everything that you don't want anymore. Which one will you pick?

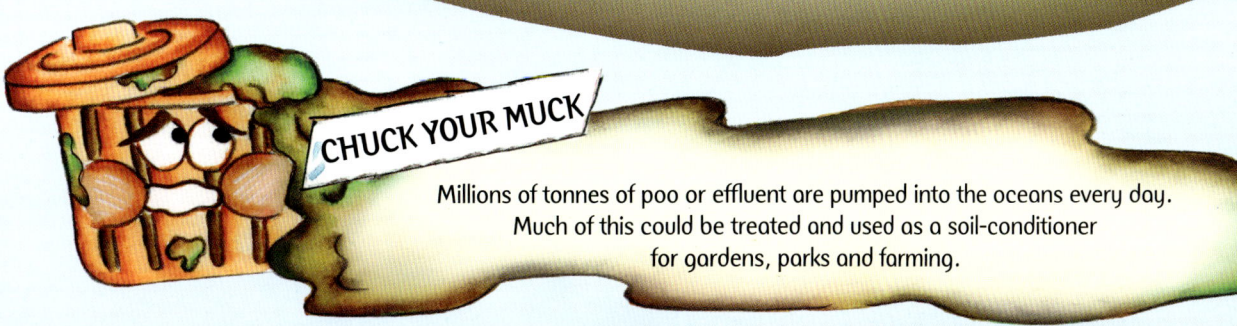

CHUCK YOUR MUCK

Millions of tonnes of poo or effluent are pumped into the oceans every day. Much of this could be treated and used as a soil-conditioner for gardens, parks and farming.

What do you throw away each day?

Living beings, depend on a supply of natural resources like sunshine, water, minerals, air, plants and soil – all essential for life as we know it.

While some natural resources are renewable, so they can be replaced, others are non-renewable and can't be replaced as quickly as they are used up. Your house, school, your favourite book, (this one), what you ate and drank last night – all started as a resource in nature. When you chuck your muck or trash your stash, natural resources are being thrown away. Dumpi and the gang have been counting resources. They reckon that unless you are an astronaut or have plans to move to the moon, there's nowhere else to look for more resources if we use them up here.

Honey... who shrank the planet?

200 years ago there were fewer than 10 million people, however, now the world population has increased to more than six billion. The first rule at recycling school is Dumpi's Dilemma©, 'If you only have one planet and an increasing population, each person must reduce their amount of world-wide waste or else… .'

Each year, the western world creates approximately 400 million tonnes of 'trash': two kilos of rubbish per person each day. That might not sound very much but if you put it all into one tonne trucks, (three metres long) and stood them end to end, the line would reach almost 12,000,000 kms – that's to the moon and back – and back to the moon again.

As the human population continues to grow, where will all the rubbish go once landfills are full?

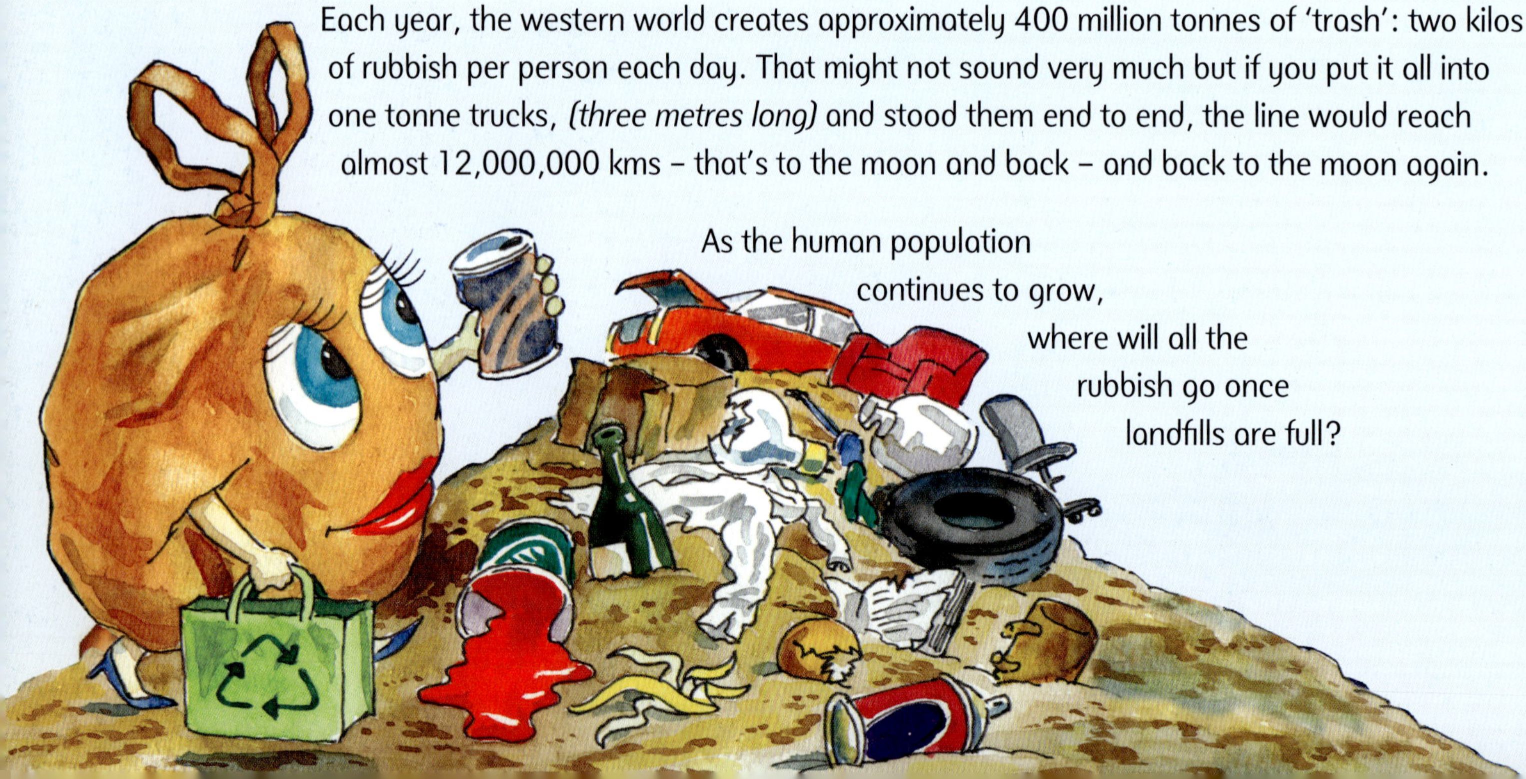

Who's a Bigfoot?

Have you examined your feet recently? Scientists have invented a way to measure your impact on our planet. It's called your ecological footprint; so sit down, take off those shoes and socks and let's check out your feet.

An ecological footprint measures the amount of energy, water, food and other resources, used up to maintain your lifestyle.

Ever had a day when nothing seems to fit?

Everything you do: open the fridge, flush the toilet, take a holiday or turn on the light, uses up natural resources. That's fine if the amount you use up is replaced at the same rate – but unfortunately, most people are using up resources faster than they can be replaced.

The current human footprint is 20% more than the planet can replace or regenerate. That's bad because it means it will take over one year and two months, for the Earth to regenerate what is used up in a single year. It just doesn't add up.

Imagine a giant ice-cream which will last forever – if you all take only three licks a day. If even just a few of you decide you want more and take five licks a day, the ice-cream will soon be… GONE!

The good news is that whilst you can't make your walking feet smaller, you can reduce your eco-footprint. It's called living sustainably. Scientists say that a smaller footprint would help save the planet's resources, reduce waste and pollution and improve everyone's quality of life, both now and in the future. So how do you shrink your footprint?

No… buying shoes that are too small won't help.

Are you a Super Poolooter?

World-wide waste is more than the stuff you chuck, the things you bin and the goo you poo. When there is too much waste it cannot be converted back into useful materials. Instead it turns into pollution.

With more than six billion people, it is impossible not to have some pollution, but humans have gone overboard and are now super poolooters. *What a great group effort!*

Unfortunately, the pollution produced by every-day activities is destroying the forces that keep Planet Earth in balance. Nature's *'Super Cycle'* can't keep up. As they say in space… *'Houston… we have a problem.'*

Let's clear up something right now. Huge amounts of pollution are produced by nature without any human help. Volcanoes, forest fires, hurricanes and wind storms all create huge particle clouds that are carried through the air. While pollution caused by natural disaster is unavoidable, air pollution created by humans… is quite a different story.

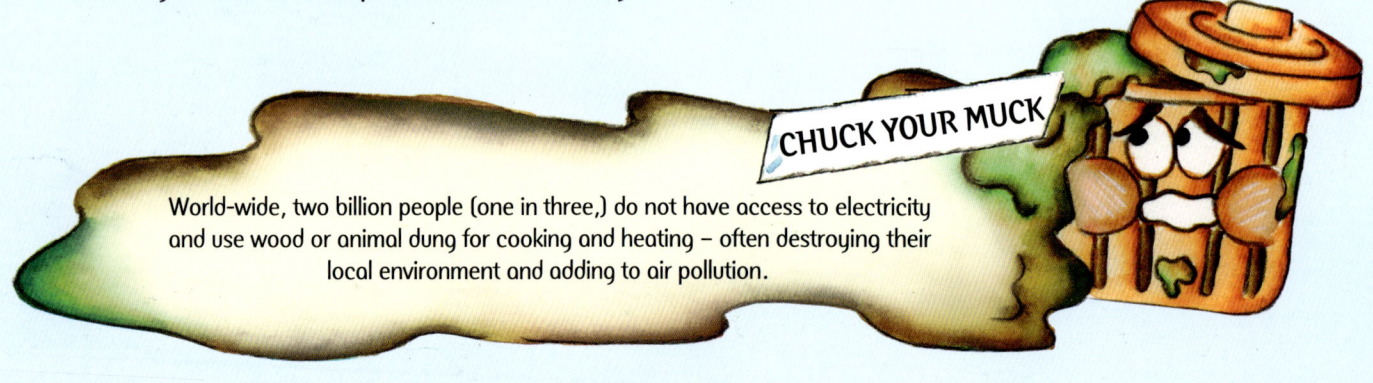

CHUCK YOUR MUCK

World-wide, two billion people (one in three,) do not have access to electricity and use wood or animal dung for cooking and heating – often destroying their local environment and adding to air pollution.

Cooking the Planet

Each year, billions of tonnes of fossil fuels - coal, oil and natural gas - are mined and extracted from under the earth's surface to provide energy for industry, homes and transport.

Energy is the building block that keeps our modern world running, and at the moment, most of that energy comes from fossil fuel. Fossil or carbon-based fuels are stored sunshine - energy from the days of the dinosaurs; created from the decomposition of prehistoric animals and plants.

Catching rays began millions of years ago

Fossil fuels produce huge amounts of easy-to-use power, but they also release greenhouse gases and other harmful wastes into the atmosphere. You can't see these wastes, but today, scientists believe that wastes released from burning fossil fuels are affecting the weather and making the planet warmer. Fossil fuel is used everyday in hundreds of ways. For example, what did you have for breakfast - cereal perhaps? How much fossil fuel energy is needed to put cereal into the millions of bowls around the world?

Planting and harvesting the grain in the cereal needs machinery that runs on fossil fuel; more fuel is needed to make fertilisers, used to grow the crop.

Packaging and shipping uses more energy. How much fuel is needed to run the truck that delivered the cereal to your supermarket? Do you know how the supermarket is powered? What powered the car on the drive to the supermarket? How was your spoon made? How is the milk kept cold?

Fossil fuel energy is used everywhere.

Some cereals have more energy than others

Fuelling the Weather

Humans are heating things up and not just when they want a cup of tea!

Scientists believe that the wastes produced from burning fossil fuels, cause huge amounts of carbon-dioxide to be released into the atmosphere. This, together with logging and other greenhouse gas-producing activities, such as waste incineration, cement manufacture and cows' bottom burps, is causing the planet to heat up.

Letting off steam is not as easy as it used to be

Who's getting warmed up?

The world burns approximately 1.9 billion tonnes of coal a year to generate electricity. At the moment, more than 85% of the world's energy demands are met by burning fossil fuels.

Three-quarters of human-caused emissions of carbon-dioxide are due to the combustion, or burning of fossil fuels.

The USA is home to about 6% of the world's population but produces about 25% of all greenhouse gases and consumes 26% of the world's energy.

China, India, Japan and South Korea - are responsible for 48% of the world's greenhouse gas emissions.

Australia with 20 million people produces more carbon-dioxide per person than any other country in the world.

The amount of carbon-dioxide in the atmosphere is up by 27% on any previous high in the last 650,000 years.
US Science Journal 2005

Global Effects

Weather and rain patterns are changing. Nine out of ten of the warmest years on record have occurred since 1990. The *Intergovernmental Panel on Climate Change* estimates global temperatures could rise by 6°C this century. A degree or two sounds tiny, but the consequences are gigantic because water expands when it heats up, increasing floods and storm surges.

Learning to swim may become a crucial part of life

50 million people a year are affected by flooding from hurricanes and storms; if the seas rise by half a metre, this number could double. A metre rise in sea-level would flood 1% of Egypt, 6% of the Netherlands and 17.5% of Bangladesh. The low-level coastal areas of Pakistan, India, Sri Lanka, Bangladesh, Burma and many of the Pacific Islands could completely disappear.

In the Hindu Kush region and Tibetan Himalayas, glacial lakes may burst their banks, flooding millions of people living in the valleys below.

Fresh water demand has tripled in the last 50 years, but temperature increases have reduced consumable water as water-tables drop, rivers die and glaciers retreat.

Animals are also affected. More than 20% of the North Pole Ice Cap has melted away in the last 25 years, reducing the ice-fields where penguins, polar bears and seals live and feed. Some scientists say that polar bears could be extinct by the end of this century.

If waste levels rise, the planet will continue to heat up. How can you help prevent this? First, turn the page and meet your greatest opponent.

Don't mess with reality... realise the gravity

Driving up Pollution

The fossil fuel waste created and sent out into our atmosphere is good news for only one guy. Meet global enemy No.1, *(a.k.a. POO-looter)* who says he's run off his feet with all the work he's got on.

Motor vehicles guzzling fossil fuels have become a major source of greenhouse gas emissions. POO-looter's biggest joy in life is hanging around, creating dust and chewing the dirt; cheering on millions of cars as they spew deadly gas into the air.

POO-looter has recently become busy in China and India, where population growth and car sales are increasing at a huge rate. In China, bicycles, which only a few years ago were the main form of transport, have been replaced by streets jammed with cars.

On the other side of the planet, Mexico City is considered the most polluted city in the world. On some days, cars have to be ordered off the roads, factories forced to reduce output, and school children are not allowed to play outside. The air is so dirty that children, when asked to paint a picture of the sky, painted it grey.

How can we stop all the waste and pollution from car emissions?

There are two options - either stop using cars, or perhaps, start using cars that run more efficiently.

Then, we could send POO-looter on the holiday he deserves and tackle world-wide waste.

CHUCK YOUR MUCK

An oil reservoir is not some vast underground lake, but a seemingly solid layer of rock that is spongy or porous. Oil fields have been found on every continent, except Antarctica

Get Behind the Wheel

Here are some options we've been test-driving, so POO-looter can take a break.

The hybrid car: Toyota™ and Honda™ have already introduced hybrids for all occasions and in many colours, *so no excuses!* Using a mixture of technologies such as internal combustion engines, electric motors, petrol and batteries, the hybrid means that cars won't guzzle as much petrol. That's great news for the atmosphere.

Fancy a ride to work?

Water-wheels: have you ever seen a car that can run on water? Hydrogen cars are less polluting than petrol-powered cars and when you burn hydrogen in an engine, water comes out of the exhaust pipe.

Anyone for salad? There are cars on the road that run on used vegetable oil. Is it a dream? No… biodiesel is made from vegetable oil. It has low emissions and can be used in diesel engines.

Getting there on air. The compressed air car is powered by AIR stored in tanks under the car. If you ran out of fuel perhaps you could just blow into the tanks?

Fuel cell technology is another clean, sustainable way to power a car. Fuel cells started as part of the space programme. They operate like batteries and combine hydrogen with oxygen to create electricity. What comes out of the exhaust is pure water - so clean that astronauts on the space shuttle can drink the water produced from their fuel cells.

SLIM YOUR BIN

Catalytic converters fitted into car exhausts reduce many of the toxic fumes from fossil fuel cars.

The Dark Side:
Fiendish Friends of SOx, COx and NOx

These pollutants are produced from burning fossil fuels. Can you help to reduce their use?

Carbon dioxide (CO_2) a.k.a **COx** is the principle greenhouse gas emitted from burning coal, oil and natural gas.

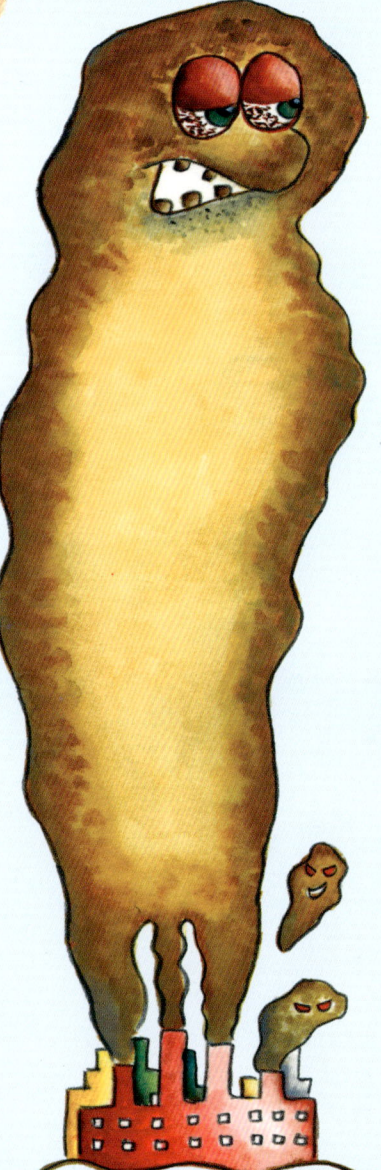

Nitrogen oxides (NOx) cause smog and acid rain. They are produced by burning petrol, diesel, and coal.

Sulphur oxides (SOx) are gases produced by burning coal, mainly in power plants and from some industrial processes, such as paper production, smelting of metals and cement manufacturing. They are major contributors to smog and acid rain which can kill entire lakes and forests.

Suspended particulate matter (SPM) consists of solids in the air in the form of smoke, dust, and vapour. These can remain suspended for extended periods and are the main source of haze which reduces visibility. The finer of these particles, when breathed in, can cause lung damage and breathing problems.

Ozone (O_3) occurs naturally in the upper layers of the atmosphere, shielding the earth from the harmful ultraviolet rays of the sun. At ground level, it is a pollutant with highly toxic effects. Vehicles and industry are the major sources of ground-level ozone emissions.

Carbon monoxide (CO) is a colourless, odourless gas produced by the incomplete burning of carbon fuels.

Lead (Pb) was widely used in petrol, diesel, lead batteries, paints and hair dye products. It can cause nervous system damage, digestive problems and even cancer.

Things that pollute the air may not be bad in themselves. Ozone is a real problem at street level, but in the stratosphere it protects us from ultraviolet rays. Lead is another example – it's a durable, easily worked metal - ideal for waterproofing a roof or screening against X-rays, but very nasty when it gets into your bloodstream.

Are you fuel-hardy?
Shrink your eco-footprint – here's how...

Your feet ARE your ride... do you really need to get a lift everywhere? Hike or ride your bike... two great ways to cut fuel emissions.

TAKE a bus or a train. Using public transport reduces pollution by limiting the number of pollution-emitting cars on the road.

What do you do in the loo? Save a full flush for a *Number Two*. Reduce paper waste and don't use six sheets of toilet paper when one will do!

WHO'S a bright spark? Is your home's electricity bill the same amount as this time last year? Can you make it lower by using energy efficient light bulbs, shower heads and electrical equipment? Turn off lights and computers when not in use and shut the fridge door.

Don't be a drip. Save Water... are you recycling any of your water? Why not get a rain-water tank and collect those precious drops when it rains? In Thailand, a system that collects condensing dew from the rooftops is providing enough water to fill a small community swimming pool.

HUG a tree. Well plant one - they absorb CO_2 from the air and give off oxygen.

MAKE a fashion statement. Recycle plastic. Plastic can be recycled into pipes, floor coverings, back-packs and even thermal boxer shorts *(for when it's chilly)*.

Is home your castle? Ask your family to install solar hot water and power systems. With some simple energy and water efficiency measures, these systems can reduce your home's contribution to greenhouse emissions and save money.

Check out a new breed. If your family is buying a car, help them choose a fuel efficient model. Hybrid cars are far more fuel efficient than a standard similar size car and can cut greenhouse gas emissions by 70 per cent.

Tell POO-looter he's an old fossil and that he should take a hike

Don't be Fuel-ish

Be a spark - come clean - think green

This planet offers many alternative, eco-friendly sources of power and energy that create little or no waste.

Hydroelectric, wind, solar, tidal and even your rubbish can be used very successfully, to create energy supplies. Energy created this way is called renewable or green energy.

Did you know that the wind has the power to create electricity? In Denmark, huge windmills power around 6,000 turbines which supply 20% of the country's total electrical power.

The sun is also a great source of energy. Solar energy taken from the sun, can replace the billions of barrels of fossil fuel oil that currently go up in smoke.

Scientists have worked out that the whole world's demand for electricity could be met today by covering a 600 square kilometre area of the Sahara desert with solar cell technology.

Rivers may look slow and sleepy but they contain an enormous amount of energy which can be converted into hydroelectric power. This renewable energy supplies 20% of the world's electricity. Iceland, Norway, Austria and Canada produce most of their electricity this way.

Let's all wave - around 75% of the earth's surface is covered in water and every wave that crashes to shore contains energy. It's limitless, free and clean: a real alternative to fossil fuel energy in the future.

What's for dinner - fancy cooking up your waste? Millions of tonnes of rubbish sent to landfills could bring power to your home just by cooking it up to a very high temperature. All sorts of rubbish can be used to provide energy – even food scraps and teabags.

Come on… time to come clean: let's look for more ways to use renewable energy and reduce wastage and our eco-footprint.

Wanting more is a bore...

Reducing waste is only half the story. The amount of resources used up also needs to be reduced.

Advertising encourages everyone to want more… and to buy things even when they are not needed. Look around. Why do people think they need a new bike, the latest mobile phone, new sneakers, a better computer or a bigger car?

Wanting more makes it easy to waste the things you already have. Next time you have a big chuck, make sure your stuff goes to a good home or gets recycled. Your trash could be someone else's treasure.

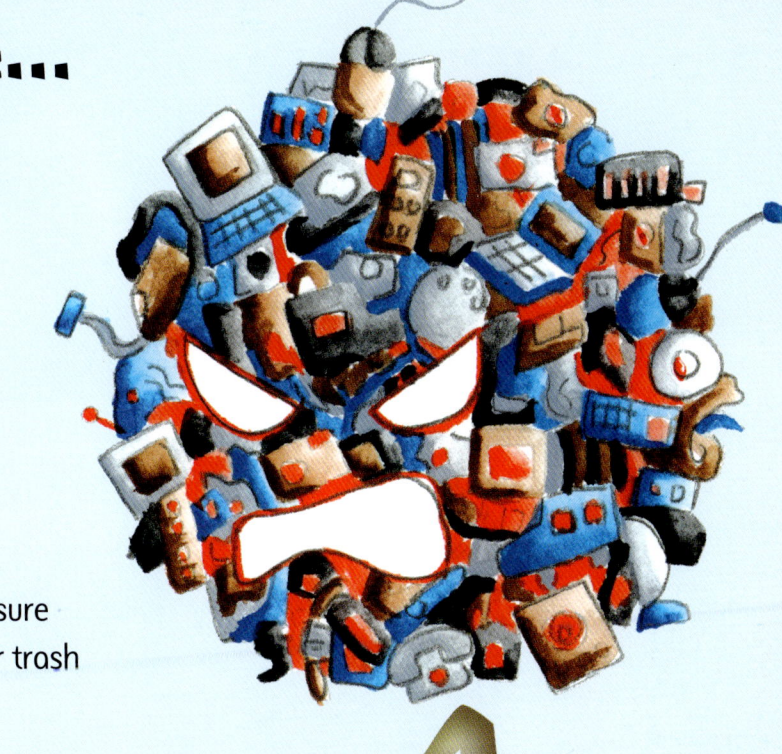

How much do you really need?

Have you noticed that the more people have, the more they want?

Around the world: 20% of people living in the highest-income countries use up 86% of all manufactured products and goods.

The richest 20% of the world
Consume 45% of all meat and fish
Consume 58% of total energy
Have 74% of all telephone lines
Consume 84% of all paper
Own 87% of the world's vehicle fleet

The poorest fifth of the world
Consume 5% of all meat and fish
Consume less than 4% of total energy
Have 1.5% of all telephone lines
Consume 1.1% of all paper
Own less than 1% of the world's vehicle fleet

Developed countries have 25% of the world's population, but consume 75% of all energy, 85% of all wood products and 72% of all the steel produced.

Between China and India, is a small country called Bhutan, where GNH is the measurement of the country's success. It stands for 'Gross National Happiness'. Perhaps if more countries measured success by happiness we could stop the buying pressure so things won't simply run out.

Open your mouth wide and say 'R'

Choosing a life-style which reduces pressure on the planet is as important as reducing waste. Don't crumple Planet Earth: it can't continue to provide water, food, light, power and shelter for everyone without your help.

When you are sick, you go to the doctor. Can you be eco-doc for Planet Earth and stop it being swamped by world-wide waste?

Help reduce wastage and give the waste you must create a second chance.

Reduce

Reducing the fossil fuel energy you use and the amount of waste you make are the best ways to reduce greenhouse gases and stop rubbish flowing into landfill.

Do you buy green power? Can you make your home more eco-friendly? What alternate energy sources can you think of?

What about the waste you throw out? Packaging makes up about half of your rubbish, so look for products that have little or no packaging.

Re-use

What you cannot reduce try to re-use. Fix or repair things rather than buying something new. You could also re-use jars and plastic containers for storage.

Green waste – that's leaves, trees, grass clippings and weeds. Don't throw them out – turn them into compost. It's great for plants, helps the soil hold water and reduces the need for chemical fertilisers.

Food waste can also be composted, adding a little variety for the microbes and worms.

Rain-water doesn't need to flow down the drain. A rain-water tank can collect the water, so it's ready for use in your garden. After all, water doesn't grow in taps.

Recycle

Recycle when you can't re-use. At the shops, ask yourself: "Can this product or its packaging be re-used or recycled? Was it produced from recycled materials?" Recycling saves energy, landfill space and resources.

Recover

Recover energy from waste. The energy that floats out into the atmosphere from chimneys and hot water pipes can be captured and used a second time around. Waste-to-energy plants work like coal-fired power plants – just with different fuel: garbage instead of coal. Waste is burned releasing heat which turns water into steam. This high-pressure steam turns the blades of a turbine generator to produce electricity that is sent to the power grid, ready for use.

Energy can also be recovered from methane gas that forms in landfills. If this is collected instead of released, it can be used as vehicle fuel or to generate electricity. *A double win - more energy and less greenhouse gases.*

Rethink & Remanufacture

Industry needs help to rethink and remanufacture their products design so they can be re-used when they are empty or finished. And you, perhaps you, YES YOU can find new ways of producing goods that use green power energy sources instead of fossil fuel?

Future Perfect

Look at these clever ideas and inventions helping to create a sustainable future and eco-friendly world. Can you invent some more?

1. Make your next car from plastic bags. Instead of being thrown out as waste, plastic can now be recycled as a raw material and used as a source of energy for making iron and steel. You might be driving a plastic bag sooner than you think!

2. Clothes made from scrap. Create your entire outfit from old plastic bottles. Did you know that it only takes five, two litre plastic bottles to make one XL T-shirt?

3. New from old. Glass jars and bottles can be collected, crushed, melted and moulded into new bottles.

4. Recycle old tyres by granulating them into fine crumbs. Crumb can be used in sports and play surfaces, carpet underlay and soles for your shoes.

5. Create art in your park. Picnic tables' seats are being made from recycled plastics and fantastic mosaic walkways can be created from broken crockery and reclaimed tiles.

6. Design a whole building. Battery-maker Duracell™ built its new international headquarters using materials from the company's own manufacturing processes: flooring made from crushed glass and broken light bulbs, ceiling tiles made from recycled newspapers and roofing made from recycled aluminium.

7. Alternate fuels. BP™ now called *Beyond Petroleum*, is the world leader in solar cells. Their new sun logo is a symbol of their shift away from fossil fuels as the main source of future energy supply.

8. Can you drink from a pencil? Plastic cups can be turned into pencils by shredding them and adding graphite, while printer cartridges can be recycled into pens. How remarkable!

9. Can't see the wood for the trees. Plastic can be converted into a wood-like material to be used for fences, garden edging, outdoor furniture and sound barriers.

10. Office paper recycled into toilet paper. You could say that it's helping get to the bottom of things…

Give Waste a Second Chance

Who's in charge? YOU ARE. Choose to use the world's resources wisely and you can reduce the trash that gets stashed. We only have one fragile planet - please don't waste it. Dumpi and the gang tell it how it is.

Dig in, fix your mix – be mean, go green

Don't mess with reality - realise the gravity
don't raise the heat - listen to the beat
and get your clan to follow the plan.
Family, friends and everyone you know,
can dig on in and fix their mix.
Starting today - just change the way you stash your trash.
Let's rock - we have a planet to save.
Come on my sisters and brothers from another mother...
give World-Wide Waste a goodbye blow,
'cos now you know... it's not just a whole load of rubbish.

Coming Clean in the 21st Century

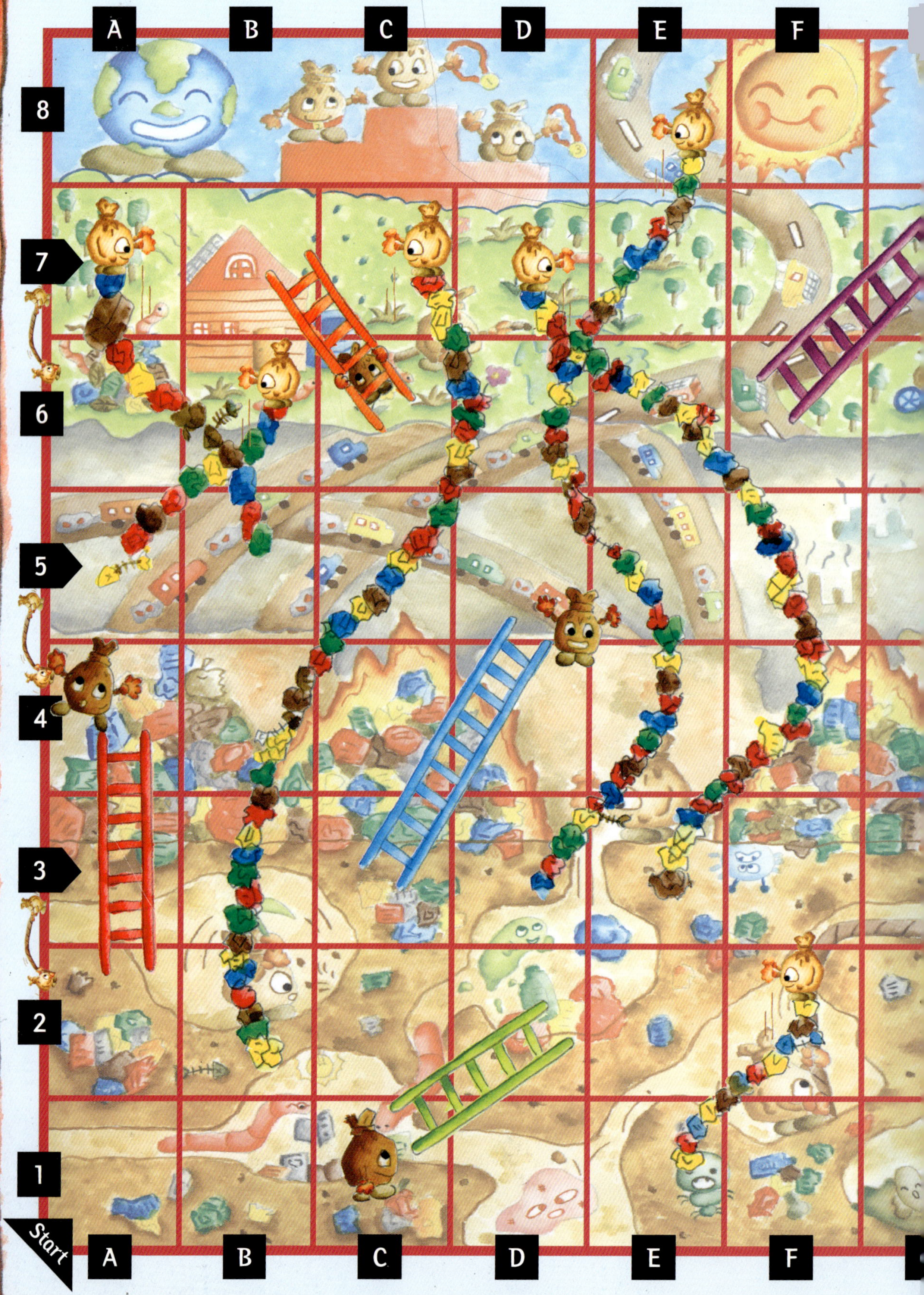

Ladders

C1 Plastic bags banned in all local supermarkets

I1 Fossil fuel replaced by green energy at petrol stations, reducing CO^2 emissions

L2 Solar hot-water systems installed in all new homes

A2 Rare munching microbe learns to eat plastic and convert it to soil

C3 New packaging is invented, strong enough to carry an elephant and 100% bio-degradable

M4 You become an architect and design a great eco-city made from recycled material

J4 Buy a really trendy outfit made from 100% plastic and win fashion award

F6 Proclaim *Eco-Footprint Day* to help spread the message that the planet is not just a giant ice-cream

C6 School science class builds machine that captures waves and converts them to electricity

K7 Install rain-water tank, grow beautiful vegetables and never run out of water